Scout and Joybell at the Show

By Eliza Webb

Scout's dad had a farm
outside town.

Scout had a pet brown hen
called Joybell.

One day, she went down
to the henhouse to see Joybell.

"You'll be in the hen show,
Joybell!" said Scout.

Scout started to groom Joybell.

She cleaned soil
from Joybell's body.

Scout cleaned Joybell's beak and mouth with a moist cloth.

Nut oil made Joybell's feet shine!

Dad and Scout took Joybell to the town showground.

Scout found a spot next to a boy with a white hen.

"It's not long now, Joybell," said Scout.

A man had a browse
in the crowded shed.
He would choose the best hen.

Some hens were rowdy and loud,
but not Joybell.

The man pointed at Joybell.

"How do you feed Joybell?"
he said.

"With roasted soy beans,"
Scout said.

"Joybell is the best hen," the man called.

"Wow!" shouted Scout.

Joybell got a big coin.

Scout felt so proud!

Dad put Joybell's coin
up on the henhouse.

I hope you enjoyed that, Joybell!

CHECKING FOR MEANING

1. What kind of animal does Scout have as a pet? *(Literal)*

2. What were three things Scout did to prepare Joybell for the hen show? *(Literal)*

3. Why do you think Joybell won the prize for best hen? *(Inferential)*

EXTENDING VOCABULARY

henhouse	What two smaller words make the word *henhouse*? How do those smaller words help you understand what a henhouse is?
rowdy	What letters in the word *rowdy* make the /ow/ sound? What does the word *rowdy* mean? How is a person or animal behaving if they are being rowdy?
proud	What does the word *proud* mean? What other emotions are related to the word *proud*? What other word in the book rhymes with *proud*?

MOVING BEYOND THE TEXT

1. Scout made sure Joybell looked her best for the hen show. Have you ever had to wash an animal? How did it go?
2. Scout felt proud of Joybell's win. When have you felt proud of achieving something?
3. What other types of animals might be found on a farm?
4. How do farmers take care of their animals to keep them healthy?

TIME TO WRITE

Write about a time when you won a prize. Or, write about something you are good at that you could win a prize for.

PRACTICE WORDS

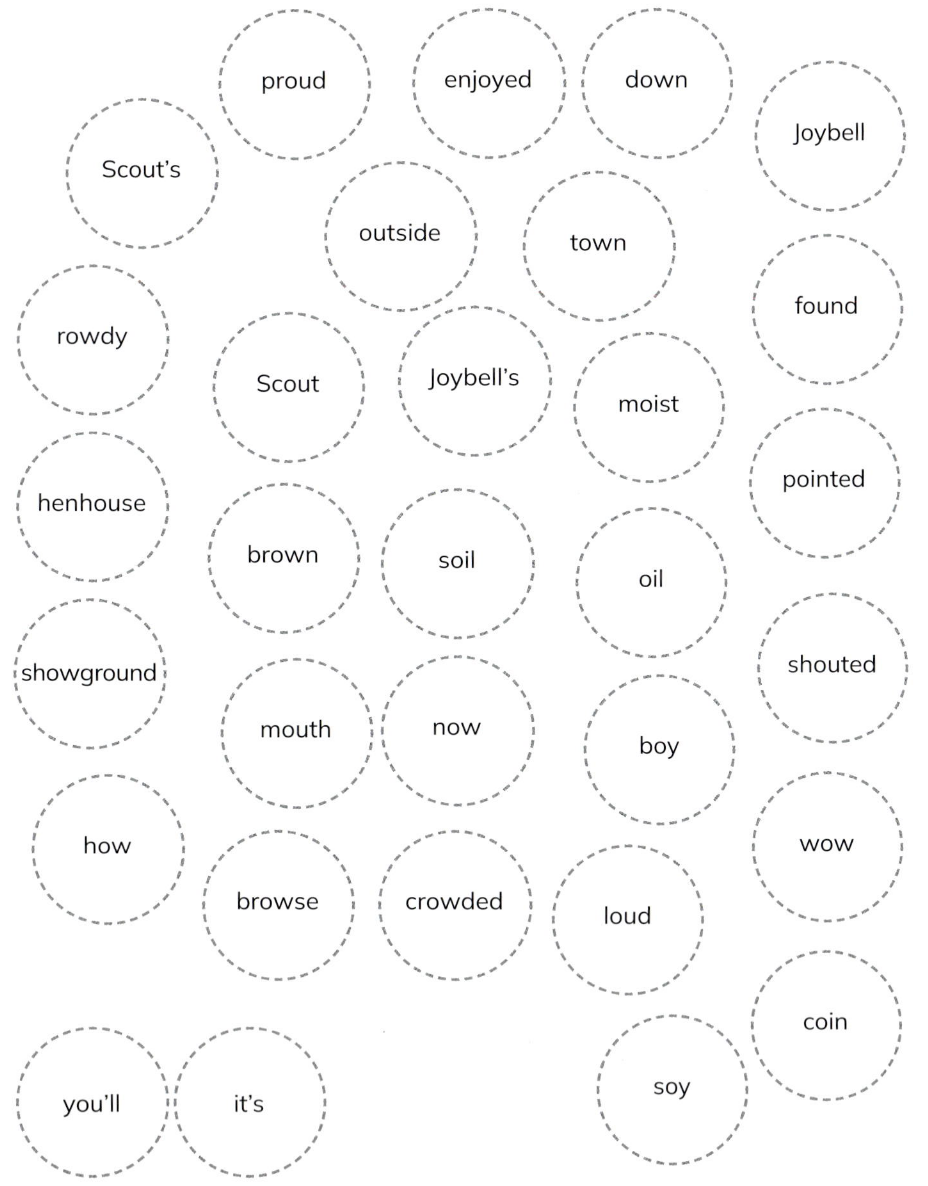